The Paintings of Peter Doig

Kevin Snowdon

Bluebell Publishing

Title Page

The Paintings of Peter Doig – Kevin Snowdon

Printed March 2020

Printed by Lulu

www.Lulu.com

ISBN: 978-1-9163546-3-0

For Amanda, Karl, Saskia

CONTENTS

Preface

Peter Doig was born 17 April 1959. Is a Scottish painter. One of the most important contemporary painters. Born in Edinburgh. As a child he lived with his family in Trinidad and Canada.

He studied art in London. Receiving an MA from Chelsea School of Art in 1990. He became a professor at the Dusseldorf Fine Arts Academy, Germany.

His paintings can be surreal and owe something to Munch and Gaugin. Art critic Jonathan Jones described his work as a "jewel of genuine imagination, sincere work and humble creativity."

Many of his paintings draw on his childhood in Canada and his time in the Caribbean. He moved back to Trinidad in 2002. Setting up the Caribbean Contemporary Arts Centre near Port of Spain. In 2007 his painting *White Canoe* sold at Sotheby's for $11.3 million.

Credits: Much of the above preface is taken from Wikipedia

The Paintings of Peter Doig

100 Years Ago

One day 100 years ago. A beautiful girl. Sat in a red canoe.
She noticed there were three plains of blue. The water. The
ice, which could be a wall. The deep azure sky to swim in.

Into these three plains of being of nature. She sailed in a
very long canoe. There where rocks or a building or New
York on the far far horizon. Trepid and brave and lost. She
gazed at you the viewer. With your lens camera and Saab car
and junk bureaucratic minds

One day 100 years ago. A princess of ice. Decided to come
and build Chicago. In the shimmering beginning of a
bathosphere of three types of blue. One day nothingness
past like the wave of a wand. And the girl travelled north.
And her gaze fell in a mirror of shimmering blue

Camp Foristia

Camp Foristia- Who lives in this house. Who will live in the house in future. Perhaps residing forever in the water reflection. In love with mirrors. In love with the mirrored. Such enchanting crisscross of tree branches in a deep dark sky. We live in this house today. Bordering the sick lime green lawn. The delicious traces of snow. Let us live in this house. Like the Walton's or Hitler or Ian Duncan Smith. Let us make interweaved stories from the windows that look out over the lake. One day we will not live there. For now shine on. In the white white palatial house over the lake.

Gasthof Zur Muldentalsperre

Celestial blue. A star fell. And exploded/evaporated/ awashed- a sea a train. Two people at a gate. The sky quivered. We drowned in love. The wall is a polka dot wedding. A fairy tale on Nantwich Cheshire. Two trees in an inundated garden. Symmetrical like a chance mirror. The two small passengers may walk through the gate as they wish and swim in the liquid blue sea of cotton wool. Or stay forever in a picture below a reverberation sky and mirrored sea.

Hitchhiker

Take a step back. From a troubled green sky. The cosy dry bright red lorry. Is heading to Chicago maybe.

The road folks near here. One route or the left route. Take a step back. See a vast large land. That may (with passports and visas and ships) curl in a sphere circle around the world

Where would you like to go? In a borrowed seat. And the flat grass meadow is sickly and under a tempestuous green sky. A verdant forest in the distance edges the road. Walk now. Stand by the road- side. And in deductive logic raise a thumb.

Miles and kilometres of travel. To the house under a new sky. Of red and scudding clouds. Within a city, you've lived in since eight years old. Five dollars in a wallet. Lakes and mountains and city motorways.

White Canoe

A white canoe. In a treasure of silver tree trunks / light blue /
black. Impossible or difficult to tell apart the sky, the land,
the water. White swishes of dappled blotches. The canoe in
a deep black lake under a deep black sky by a deep black
forest. A kaleidoscope of indiscernible rich colours.

Nobody in the painting. But the empty white canoe. And
opal/ gold/ diamond/ onyx/ amethyst/ fluorspar/ emerald.
In eighty mirrors. A person-less painting of black and an
empty canoe. Mirrored in exactitude in the black dark water.

The Architects House in a Ravine

Dappled unsolvable jigsaw of spindly tree branches. Odd orange/red bark. The last hopes of the esteemed architect ruined

A house on an anti- hill. Magnet for floods. The oh, so careful brazen architects plans. The purpose of the house. Sunk. Swallowed. Engulphed. Still we live here. Pick the cherry blossom. To make a wedding. The houses unusual considered shape sings softly. As strange birds do in the surrounding woods. One day we became dependant. Lots of small things went wrong. Three days later we crammed the car the trailer and caravan and left. The unusual Avant Garde architects house is for sale?

Boiler House

Surrounded by trees. Sequestered house. Fathomable horror and banality. Foliage. Destitute hope. None around except the dead.

Come here if you will. Do not laugh, or shout, even in pleasure. Disturb none. Can you do better than the previous residents of the boiler house. A fate so terrible. House empty 30 years. Death by tv watching. Damp floor- boards. Destitution. Dilapidation. Whispers in the virile dense wood/forest. Natures spleen.

Blotter

A child, below a pond or lake. Snow- bank. Trees stretching up a slope. White snow/ pinkish snow/ silver gold ice. The child stands in blue coat. Perhaps the ice is not that thick. And rivulets form around his feet. The ice reflects that which is around him. Light cascades in the ice over the water. The boy is alone in the painting in enchantment. Danger, is present as the boy in childhood revelry tests and looks at the ice.

Night Bathers, 2019

Night Ice bathing for those with grey skin. A woman in yellow bikini soaking up the freeing night air. Further away a man. Vast turgid green lake or sea. A white moon.

Each participant unaware of the absurdity. Or it could be Saharan sand in Mauritania. On the azure Atlantic. We would not want to join them. But next to the sand building they are strangely reassuring. Like a lizard darting into the moors heather. Like an owls soft twill when exiting the car at one in the morning.

Lapeyrouse Wall

A man with a polka dot umbrella. Ambles in the delicious citrus sun past Trinidad's main cemetery. The wall is corroded and ramshackle. Perhaps the dead come out at night and destruct the bars of their home. A wooden plank fails to mend the wall. Insouciant under sun shadows. The man like theatre goer as the Paris commune takes shape. Walks with cap on his head to his destination.

Baked

Deep red exploding textured red sea. Rocks promontories. And an air yacht. Mirroring red sky. Flecked with pearls of unexplained light dots. A sublime dawn or sunset. That engulfs and is much more overly red than a respectable suburban housing estate at 7am. Red like a car or house wall sides. But vast.

Restless City

A deep sonorous brown sky. Flayling ochre wisps of a tall plant. Yellow city. Yellow bridge. Bright red river through the two sides of the city. In the prominent foreground. In grey colours a man and a woman face each other. The man is ardent. The woman quizzical. Perhaps they discuss the status of the yellow city. Maybe they wish not to return. Or they are drawn back. Maybe there is a drama. Maybe a drama they are unaware of. And shapes in arrayed colours are inexplicably behind them. Further behind the yellow city with red river and yellow bridge.

Road House, 1991

Snow over the terse hamlet. A field of luscious red. Houses behind a tree. That leans like one person to love. Further in from the red grass is a lime green field or a river. Shrubs to the left. Other outbuildings to the house/home. It would be nice to live here unlike some other of Doig's buildings. A grey brown wall. A sky with floating snow patches and a sort of blue that no sky is. A mottled blue. It would be nice to live here and escape corona virus.

Music of the Future

Blue shimmering pond. Colourful buildings. Dark blue sky. Figures in the lawn. A Trinidad and Tobago idyll. Happy people by the shimmering lake. It took slow development of decades. To build an ensemble of dwellings for the lake. Matched wonderment. The people pedestrians on the shore.

Drinking Chinese vodka. And a speciality of orange juice and ice cream. It was easy building a hamlet by the lake. And enjoyment came as like breath. Nobody works here. On ko Balon Leh, Thailand.

But one day. We realized we missed the driven goal attainment of London. It was easy leaving. We looked at the lake. Then walked to the road. And caught a bus to Port of Spain. Then as flight to London. Over the blue shimmering Atlantic.

Orange Sunshine, 1995

Sublime orange trees. Under a pearl and apple sky. White frost on an auburn hill. Tiny people in utopia. Dancing in the trees. A sort of house or is it a blue rock

Why do we come here? To dance amongst the trees. That are in a line of firs dark orange. In the background white mountains? And more trees. Why is one man larger than the other four? We came here by salmon and arctic tern instinct. To cavort in the trees and taste snow. There is room for you. Endlessly. Under a lime and cherry sky.

Sky Jacket

White snow. In the midst a sky jacket. That doesn't actually look like a sky jacket discernably. But a mound of black triangular. Against angel wings of white. Indiscernible. And pools of grey

But oh the swished glide through the slalom of trees. The deep powder snow. The greenery of firs. The white angelic blue mountains. The café we drank coffee in. The white green pink of myriad hope.

Two Trees

Here in Trinidad. Leyroy is by the Caribbean ocean. As Serol and Gail join him. The trees are Gauginesque purple. A white sun or moon rises or sets. There brightly coloured clothes match their kaleidoscope souls. The sky is a wash of light lilac.

We unlike Peter Doig are not from here. But the meeting of three on the shore. Is appealing. And as old as cro magnon man. The sea continues to them. There is no shore. A blue tide. A soliloquy of words.

Pine House (Rooms for Rent) 1994

A house that you could rent. Terrible rooms. In a dead street. A river of a road. Tree overhanging. Deadened tinsel street. Vast amphitheatre of belonging. Yellowing rooms. Pink sky with trees branches. A red sash of an outside wall. Do not live here in the pine house unless for circumstances it is necessary.

About Nick Monks:

Nick Monks lives near Preston, Lancashire, UK. He studied Philosophy at Hull University.

He has travelled widely for about seven years. Worked in scores of careers. His poems have appeared in numerous UK magazines and a few international.

He is currently trying to write a novel and filmscript.